Coloring Book For Teens

Anti-Stress Designs Vol 5

ART THERAPY COLORING

Preview of Coloring Pages

Pizza Peace

Preview of Coloring Pages

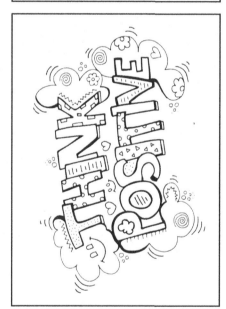

with Love

Pizza Peace

Test Your Colors

Drawings

Drawings

Drawings

Best Selling Art Therapy Coloring Books

Coloring Books For Adults:

- Zombie Coloring Book: Black Background
- Butterfly Coloring Book For Adults: Black Background
- Tattoo Coloring Book: Black Background
- Coloring Books for Adults Relaxation: Native American Inspired Designs
- Fishing Coloring Book for Adults: Black Background

Coloring Books For Men:

- Coloring Book for Men: Anti-Stress Designs Vol 1
- Coloring Book For Men: Fishing Designs
- Coloring Book For Men: Tattoo Designs
- Coloring Books for Men: Hunting
- Coloring Book For Men: Biker Designs

Coloring Books For Seniors:

- Coloring Book For Seniors: Nature Designs Vol 1
- Coloring Book For Seniors: Anti-Stress Designs Vol 1
- Coloring Books for Seniors: Relaxing Designs
- Coloring Book For Seniors: Floral Designs Vol 1
- Coloring Book For Seniors: Ocean Designs Vol 1

Coloring Books For Teens and Tweens:

- Coloring Books For Teens: Ocean Designs
- Coloring Books for Teen Girls Vol 1
- Teen Inspirational Coloring Books
- Coloring Book for Teens: Anti-Stress Designs Vol 1
- Tween Coloring Books For Girls: Cute Animals

Coloring Books For Older Kids:

- Coloring Books For Girls: Cute Animals
- Horse Coloring Book For Girls
- Coloring Books For Boys: Sharks
- Coloring Books for Boys: Animal Designs
- Unicorn Coloring Book for Girls
- Detailed Coloring Books For Kids

Art Therapy Coloring Books

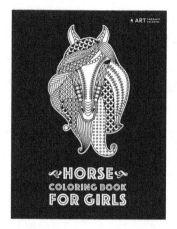

HORSE COLORING BOOK FOR GIRLS

UNICORN COLORING BOOK FOR GIRLS

COLORING BOOKS FOR GIRLS UNICORNS

COLORING BOOKS FOR GIRLS ANIMAL DESIGNS

COLORING BOOKS FOR TEEN GIRLS VOL 1 DETAILED DESIGNS

TEEN COLORING BOOKS FOR GIRLS VOL 1

TEEN COLORING BOOKS FOR GIRLS VOL 2

TEEN COLORING BOOKS FOR GIRLS VOL 3

COLORING BOOKS FOR GIRLS CUTE ANIMALS

GIRLS COLORING BOOKS CUTE ANIMALS

COLORING BOOKS FOR GIRLS ANIMALS

COLORING BOOKS FOR GIRLS Princess & Unicorn Designs

GIRLS COLORING BOOKS DETAILED DESIGNS VOL 1

COLORING BOOKS FOR GIRLS DETAILED DESIGNS VOL 2

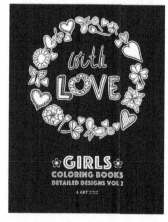

with LOVE GIRLS COLORING BOOKS DETAILED DESIGNS VOL 2

COLORING BOOKS FOR GIRLS RELAXATION «Hearts»

Art Therapy Coloring Books

COLORING BOOKS
FOR TEENS
WOLVES & MORE

~TEEN~
COLORING BOOKS
ANIMAL DESIGNS

~TEEN~
COLORING BOOKS
ANIMALS
Black Background

COLORING BOOKS
FOR TEENS
~OWLS~

~TEEN~
INSPIRATIONAL
COLORING BOOKS

~TEEN~
COLORING BOOKS
ANIMAL DESIGNS
Black Background

~DETAILED~
COLORING BOOK
FOR TEENAGERS
Animal Designs

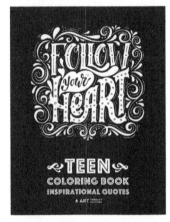

~TEEN~
COLORING BOOK
INSPIRATIONAL QUOTES

TWEEN COLORING
BOOKS FOR GIRLS
CUTE ANIMALS

ADULT COLORING BOOKS
~FOR TEENS~
Animal Designs

COLORING BOOKS
FOR TEENS
CAT & DOG DESIGNS

MANDALA
COLORING BOOK
FOR TEENS
Black Background

COLORING BOOKS
FOR TEENS
SEAHORSES & MORE

COLORING BOOKS
FOR TEENS
RELAXATION
Dolphins & More

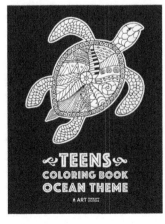

~TEENS~
COLORING BOOK
OCEAN THEME

COLORING BOOKS
FOR TEENS
SHARKS & MORE

Art Therapy Coloring Books

COLORING BOOKS
FOR BOYS
WILD ANIMALS

COLORING BOOKS
FOR BOYS
~DRAGONS~

COLORING BOOKS
FOR BOYS
ANIMAL DESIGNS

COLORING BOOKS
FOR BOYS
OCEAN DESIGNS
Black Background

COLORING BOOKS
FOR BOYS
~SHARKS~

DINOSAUR
COLORING BOOKS
FOR BOYS
Detailed Designs

COLORING BOOKS
FOR BOYS
NATIVE AMERICAN INSPIRED

COLORING
BOOKS FOR BOYS
ANIMALS

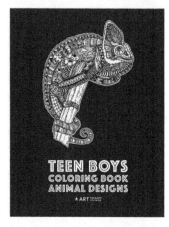

TEEN BOYS
COLORING BOOK
ANIMAL DESIGNS

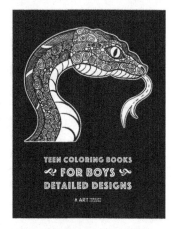

TEEN COLORING BOOKS
~ FOR BOYS ~
DETAILED DESIGNS

TEEN COLORING BOOKS
~ FOR BOYS ~
DETAILED DESIGNS
Black Background

COLORING BOOKS
FOR TEEN BOYS
DETAILED DESIGNS

COLORING BOOKS
FOR TEEN BOYS
DETAILED DESIGNS
Black Background

ADULT
COLORING BOOKS
FOR KIDS
Geometric Designs

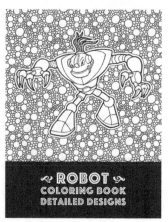

~ROBOT~
COLORING BOOK
DETAILED DESIGNS

DETAILED
COLORING BOOKS
FOR KIDS

Art Therapy Coloring Books

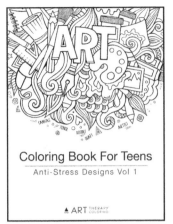

Coloring Book For Teens

Anti-Stress Designs Vol 1

▲ ART THERAPY COLORING

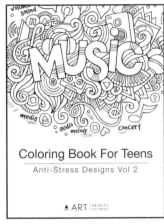

Coloring Book For Teens

Anti-Stress Designs Vol 2

▲ ART THERAPY COLORING

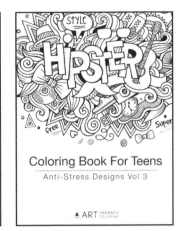

Coloring Book For Teens

Anti-Stress Designs Vol 3

▲ ART THERAPY COLORING

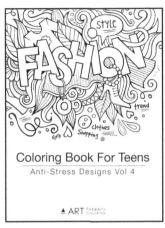

Coloring Book For Teens

Anti-Stress Designs Vol 4

▲ ART THERAPY COLORING

Coloring Book For Teens

Anti-Stress Designs Vol 5

▲ ART THERAPY COLORING

Coloring Book For Teens

Anti-Stress Designs Vol 6

▲ ART THERAPY COLORING

Coloring Book For Teens

Anti-Stress Designs Vol 7

▲ ART THERAPY COLORING

Coloring Book For Teens

Anti-Stress Designs Vol 8

▲ ART THERAPY COLORING

Teen Coloring Book

Stress Relieving Designs

▲ ART THERAPY COLORING

Tween Coloring Book

Animal Designs Vol 1

▲ ART THERAPY COLORING

Stay ✦ Wild!

Tween Coloring Book

Animal Designs Vol 2

▲ ART THERAPY COLORING

Tween Coloring Books For Girls

Stress Relief Vol 1

▲ ART THERAPY COLORING

Tween Coloring Books For Girls

Stress Relief Vol 2

▲ ART THERAPY COLORING

Tween Coloring Book

I Love You!!!

▲ ART THERAPY COLORING

Tween Coloring Book

Wolves, Lions, Tigers

▲ ART THERAPY COLORING

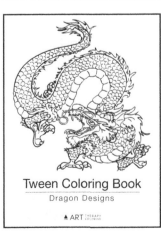

Tween Coloring Book

Dragon Designs

▲ ART THERAPY COLORING

Coloring Book For Teens
Anti-Stress Designs Vol 5

Published by:
Art Therapy Coloring
www.arttherapycoloring.com

Images Licensed by Shutterstock

ISBN: 978-1-944427-20-7

Made in United States
North Haven, CT
07 April 2023

35159729R00050